SCIENCE WORKSHOP

MAGNETISM

Pam Robson

GLOUCESTER PRESS

NEW YORK CHICAGO LONDON SYDNEY

Design   David West
                  Children's Book Design
Editor   Suzanne Melia
Designer   Steve Woosnam-Savage
Picture Researcher Emma Krikler
Illustrator   Ian Thompson
Consultant   Geoff Leyland

First published in
the United States in 1993 by
Gloucester Press
95 Madison Avenue
New York, NY 10016

© Aladdin Books Ltd 1992

Library of Congress
Cataloging-in-Publication Data

  Robson, Pam
     Magnetism / Pam Robson.
       p.   cm. — (Science workshop)
     Includes index.
     Summary: Explores the properties
  of magnets and ways to work with the
  forces of attraction and repulsion.
     ISBN 0-531-17399-2
     1. Magnetism—Juvenile literature.
  2. Magnetism—Experiments—
  Juvenile literature. [1. Magnetism—
  Experiments. 2. Experiments.] I. Title.
  II. Series.
  QC753.7.R6 1993
  538'.078—dc20   92-37098   CIP

CONTENTS

PHOTOCREDITS

All the photographs in this book are by Roger
Vlitos apart from pages; 18 top: Mary Evans
Picture Library; 20 top and 28 top: Science
Photo Library; 22 top right: Popperfoto.

INTRODUCTION

Magnetism is a force that acts between magnets. You may think of magnets as toys that pick up nails or other bits of iron and steel, but magnetism is an important force in nature. Magnetism is all around us and we use it every day. Magnets come in all shapes and sizes. Magnets are used in telephones, television sets, and radios; they can work giant machines, they can seek out North in direction, and they can push and pull other magnets. In fact, the world has become a different place since magnetism was first discovered. People once believed that magnets had mystical powers and could heal the sick. It was when sailors first learned how to magnetize a compass needle, however, that the age of science began. The Magnetic North Pole of the earth was located in 1831 by Sir James Clark Ross, and almost 100 years later, in 1909, the Magnetic South Pole was located by a party led by Lord Shackleton. Today, we know much more about the earth and magnetism. We even rely on magnetism to produce large amounts of electricity for us. As you find out more about magnetism and magnets, you will discover that they are not only very useful, but a great deal of fun too!

Introduction

Bright Ideas for further projects

Science projects with practical experiments

Why it Works explaining the science ideas

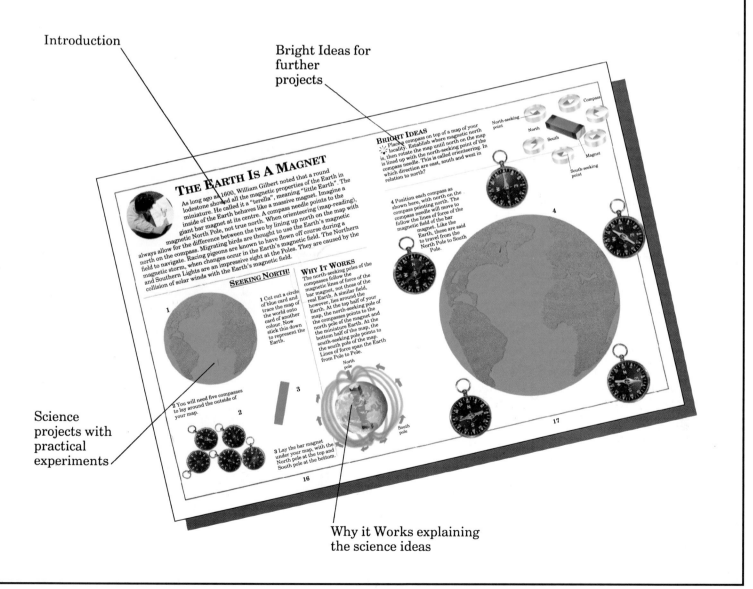

THE WORKSHOP

A science workshop is a place to test ideas, perform experiments, and make discoveries. To prove many scientific facts you don't need a lot of fancy equipment. In fact, everything you need for a basic workshop can be found around your home or school. Read through these pages and then use your imagination to add to your "home laboratory." Make sure that you are aware of relevant safety rules and look after the environment. A science experiment is an activity that involves the use of certain basic rules to test a hypothesis. A qualitative approach involves observation. A quantitative approach involves measurement. Remember, one of the keys to being a creative scientist is to keep experimenting. This means experimenting with equipment as well as with ideas, to give you the most accurate results. In this way, you will build up your workshop as you go along.

MAKING THE MODELS

Before you begin, read through all the steps. Then make a list of the things you need and gather them together. Next, think about the project so that you have a clear idea of what you are about to do. Finally, take your time in putting the pieces together. You will find that your projects work best if you wait while glue or paint dries. If something goes wrong, retrace your steps. And, if you can't fix it, start over again. Every scientist makes mistakes, but the best ones know when to begin again!

GENERAL TIPS

There are at least two parts to every experiment: experimenting with materials and testing a science "fact." If you don't have all the materials, experiment with others instead. For example, if you can't find any sand, use sawdust or shredded paper instead. Once you've finished experimenting, read your notes thoroughly and think about what happened, evaluating your measurements and observations. See what conclusions you can draw from your results.

SAFETY WARNINGS

Make sure that an adult knows what you are doing at all times. Filing an iron nail to make iron filings can be dangerous. Ask an adult to do this for you. In the experiments that use electricity, always use a battery of 1.5 volts. Never use main-line electricity! Always be careful with scissors. If you spill any water, wipe it up right away. Slippery surfaces are dangerous. Clean up your workshop when you finish!

EXPERIMENTING

Always conduct a "fair test." This means changing one thing at a time for each stage of an experiment. In this way, you can always tell which change caused a different result. As you go along, record what you see and compare your results with what you thought would happen before you began. Ask questions such as "why?" "how?" and "what if?" Then test your project and write down the answers you find. Compare your results to those of your friends or classmates.

MAGNETIC ATTRACTION

Archaeologists and beachcombers often make use of metal detectors to locate buried objects or treasure. Materials are either magnetic or nonmagnetic. Most, but not all, metals are magnetic. Iron has the strongest magnetic attraction. Nickel and cobalt are also magnetic, as are the alloys, or mixtures, of these metals. Aluminum, copper, and gold are nonmagnetic. Magnetic ferrites (metals containing iron) can be used to make hard magnets, like the refrigerator magnets pictured here. These are known as permanent magnets. Soft magnets are temporary and are easy to magnetize and demagnetize. Magnetic materials can be easily separated from other materials. When aluminum cans are recycled, they are sorted from other metals by using a magnet. You can make your own metal detector with an ordinary magnet. See if you can find any buried treasure!

SECRETS IN THE SAND

2 Hold the cone in place by attaching small strips of paper to it and winding them tightly around the stick. Now decorate the cone with paint or colored paper.

1

2

1 Make a circle, 4 inches across out of colored cardboard and cut a slit from the edge to the center. Overlap the two ends and glue, to create a flat cone. Push one end of a stick through the center and attach a button magnet to the stick with clay.

3 Half fill a shallow container with clean sand. Bury a variety of objects in the sand, metals and nonmetals.

4 Move your metal detector slowly above the surface of the sand. Try it at various heights. You will soon discover how low you must hold it to attract objects.

3

WHY IT WORKS

A magnet exerts a force on a nearby piece of magnetic material by turning it into a weak magnet – this is magnetic induction. A magnet is made up of many tiny parts called domains. Each one is like a mini-magnet, and they all point in the same direction. The domains in a metal are jumbled up. When a magnet comes into contact with the metal, the domains line up and the metal becomes magnetized. A strong magnet can act over quite a distance. Each object picked up from the sand is a temporary magnet because the domains inside become aligned.

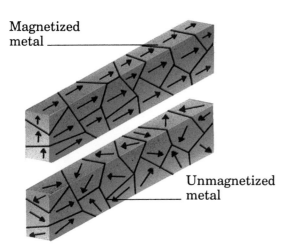

Magnetized metal

Unmagnetized metal

BRIGHT IDEAS

💡 Predict which objects you expect your magnet to pick up - you may be surprised! See how near to the sand the magnet must be held before it picks anything up. At what height does it fail to attract any of the hidden objects? Keep a record of your results.

💡 Which objects does your magnet pick up? Which are left buried in the sand? What does this tell you about them? (Hint: the answer is on this page.) Notice whether any of the magnetic objects keep their magnetism and attract other objects.

💡 Try a different kind of magnet. See if you can pick up any more objects with it. See what happens if you add more sand to the container.

💡 Find out which other metals are non-magnetic. Collect some empty drink cans and sort them with a magnet. Remember, aluminum is nonmagnetic. Save the cans for recycling.

4

WHERE IS MAGNETISM?

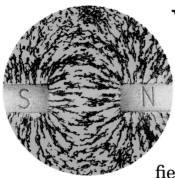

Magnetite, or lodestone, is a naturally occurring magnetic ferrite. The first magnets were made by stroking magnetic materials with a lodestone. You will find magnets of many shapes and sizes – bar, horseshoe, and button are only a few. Every magnet is surrounded by something called a magnetic field, wherever magnetism is found. The areas of the magnet where magnetism is at its strongest are called the poles. Every magnet has at least two poles. Poles are named after the direction they point in. These are North and South.

Iron filings

FLAT FIELDS

1 Place two bar magnets beneath a large sheet of paper, resting each end of the paper on a thin book. Position the magnets with unlike poles facing each other.

2

2 Ask a grown-up to make some iron filings by filing down an iron nail. Now scatter them over the surface of the paper, around the positions of both magnets. Tap the paper gently and watch the magnetic fields form.

WHY IT WORKS

Magnetic lines of force run from north to south and they are strongest where the lines are closest together. This indicates where the poles of the magnet are located. Because like poles repel, for example two south poles, the magnetic fields of the magnets also repel each other. As the iron filings are magnetized they are drawn into the magnetic field, showing the lines of force around the magnet.

BRIGHT IDEAS

Move the two magnets so that like poles are facing each other. Notice that the shape of the magnetic field has changed.

Repeat the experiment with magnets of different shapes and observe the pattern of the magnetic field of each.

Hit a magnet with a hammer – notice what effect this has on the magnet. See if you can still show its magnetic field with the iron filings.

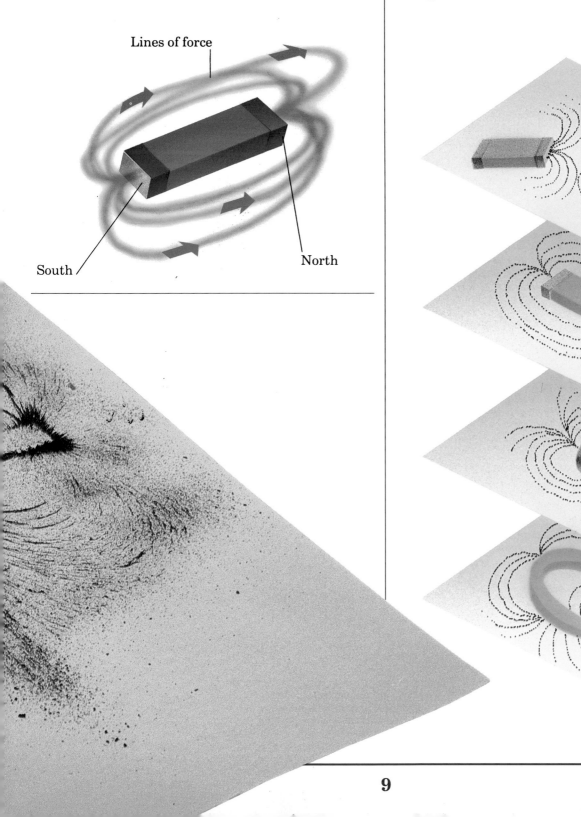

Lines of force

South

North

MAGNETIC FIELDS

The space around a permanent magnet in which its effects can be felt is called its magnetic field. A permanent magnet exerts a force that extends some distance from it in every direction. These invisible lines are like closed loops, with part of the loop inside the magnet and part forming the field outside. The lines of force never touch or cross. You have already seen how iron filings give a flat picture of a magnetic field. A magnetic field can cause a compass needle, which is itself a bar magnet, to move. The presence of a magnet near electrical equipment can create havoc, in the same way as the magnetic needle in a compass is made to move. Magnetic shields are designed to avoid such problems (see page 14). Using iron filings and oil you can demonstrate the three-dimensional nature of a magnetic field.

OIL FIELDS

1 Fill a see-through container almost to the top with a clear, thick liquid like cooking oil or glycerine. Scatter iron filings into the liquid and gently stir the mixture with a stick to disperse the filings evenly.

1

2 Now place a bar magnet underneath the jar and allow the filings to settle. View them from above. You will see the magnetic field of the magnet as a three-dimensional pattern formed by the iron filings.

10

BRIGHT IDEAS

Try holding a horseshoe magnet against the outside of the jar. See what effect this has on the iron filings in the oil. Notice where the lines of force are closest together.

Jar

Oil

Iron filings

2

WHY IT WORKS

The iron filings become temporary magnets while inside the magnetic field of the bar magnet, bunching together where the field is strongest. The oil supports the filings in the shape they form around the magnet. The lines of force in a magnetic field move from north to south. Every magnet has a North and South pole at each end, like the earth. As you can see from the shape appearing in the oil, magnetic lines of force are closest at the poles – this is where the magnet is strongest. The weakest part of a magnet is at its center.

ATTRACTION AND REPULSION

Within its magnetic field a magnet will either attract or repel another magnet. If two metal objects attract each other, it is difficult to tell which one is the magnet. The only true test of a magnet is to see if it is repelled by another magnet. A bar magnet has two poles, one North and one South. If a bar magnet is broken in the middle, new poles will appear at the broken ends. As we know that like poles repel and unlike poles attract, it is wrong to describe the North-seeking point of a compass needle as "North." In fact, it is the South pole of the magnetic needle that is attracted to the earth's magnetic North Pole. Always use the term "North-seeking" to avoid confusion. Using the laws of magnetic attraction and repulsion, see if you can move a toy car around the track. The attraction and repulsion between the two magnets should be strong enough to push and pull the car. Maybe you can win a race!

TRACK EVENT

1

1 Firmly attach a bar magnet to the roof of a toy car. Use some strong tape. Make sure that the magnet is well balanced.

2 Cut out a racetrack from gray cardboard and attach it with glue to a sheet of green cardboard – make sure there are no bumps. Add some trees.

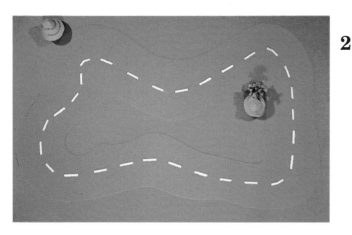

2

3 Place the car on the track. Hold one end of a bar magnet close to the end of the magnet at the rear of the car. If the car moves backward turn the magnet you are holding around the other way. You can push or pull the car around the track by holding the magnet in different places.

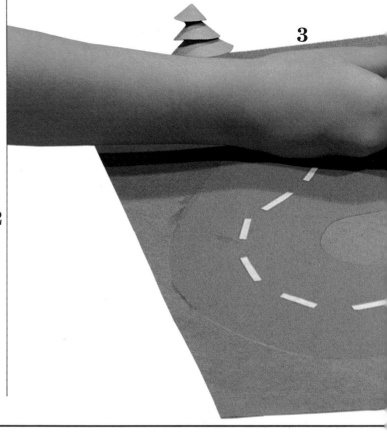

3

WHY IT WORKS

Magnets can push or pull because like poles repel but unlike poles attract. This attraction and repulsion is strong enough to push and pull the car around the track.

When two north poles face each other the opposing magnetic fields cancel each other out – this is called the neutral point. The repulsion between two like poles can be so strong that it is impossible to push them together. This magnetic force can be used to push the toy car around the track. In the same way, the attraction between opposite poles can be used to drag the car along.

BRIGHT IDEAS

Suspend a small magnet above a needle attached by thread to a flat surface. Watch the needle rise up into the air.

Suspend a bar magnet freely. Close to it suspend a second magnet. Watch them move as the like poles pull away from each other.

North

South

South

North

South

North

North

South

Straw

Thread

Magnet

Modeling clay

Needle

Thread

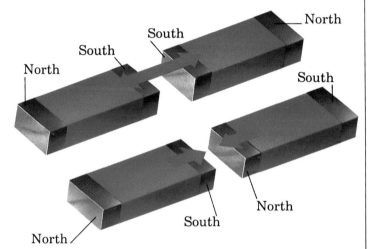

MAGNETISM TRAVELS

A magnetic force can travel through many substances. It can even travel through water. Treasure on the seabed can be detected by a diver carrying an instrument called a magnetometer. The same is true of other nonmagnetic materials – you have already seen how magnetic lines of force can travel through paper to the iron filings. What other materials do you think magnetism could travel through? Because tiny magnets as fine as powder are used to store images and sounds on tapes and computer disks, a magnetic field can interfere with the quality. The effect can only be lessened by placing another magnetic object within the magnetic field. This is a shield that cancels out the effect. Make this hockey game and prove that magnetism can travel through nonmagnetic materials.

FACE-OFF!

1 Cut out two figures holding hockey sticks from cardboard. Color them so that they are wearing different shirts. Behind each hockey stick attach a small magnet with modeling clay.

2 Attach a bar magnet firmly to one end of two long sticks. These sticks can then be held underneath the "rink" and used to move the players.

3 The hockey rink can be made from a painted cardboard lid raised up on four wooden legs. Fold two strips of cardboard to be the goalposts. Mark the center line and circles with colored tape. Put the "players" in position, facing each other. You can score goals using a Ping-Pong ball.

WHY IT WORKS

Nonmagnetic materials allow a magnetic field to pass through them. A magnetic material will pick up the magnetic force and weaken it. Cardboard is not magnetic. It allows a magnetic force to pass through it. Distance is important. If the magnet is too far away or if the nonmagnetic material is too thick, the effect of the magnet will not be felt. Some magnets are stronger than others. The weaker the magnet, the closer it must be held to the magnetic material. A strong magnet can be held further away because its magnetic field is larger.

BRIGHT IDEAS

Fill a plastic see-through container with water and attach a paper clip to the bottom with modeling clay, as shown. Now take a cork and insert another paper clip to make a hook. Using a bar magnet on the outside of the container, see if you can drag the cork to the bottom and anchor it to the clip. See what other materials magnetism will work through. Try plastic, wood, and china.

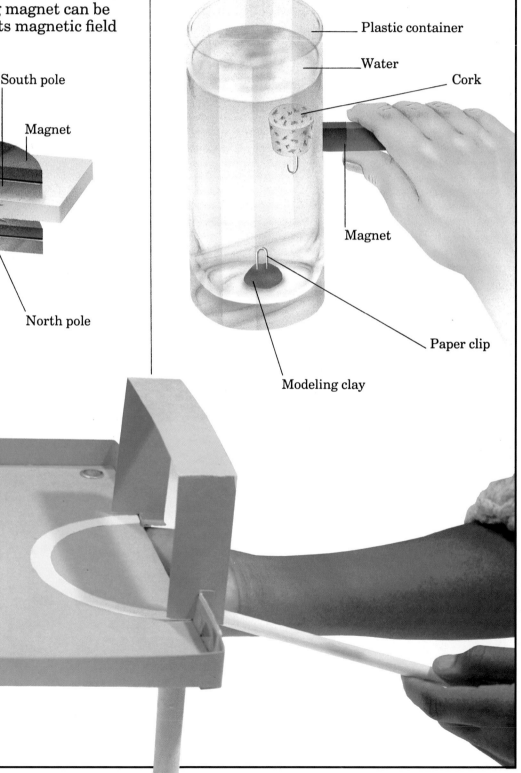

South pole

Magnet

Cardboard

Magnet

North pole

Plastic container

Water

Cork

Magnet

Paper clip

Modeling clay

15

THE EARTH IS A MAGNET

As long ago as 1600, William Gilbert noted that a round lodestone showed all the magnetic properties of the earth in miniature. He called it a "terella," meaning "little earth." The inside of the earth behaves like a massive magnet. Imagine a giant bar magnet at its center. A compass needle points to the magnetic North Pole, not true north. When orienteering (mapreading), always allow for the difference between the two by lining up north on the map with north on the compass. Migrating birds are thought to use the earth's magnetic field to navigate. Racing pigeons are known to fly off course during a magnetic storm, when changes occur in the earth's magnetic field. The Northern and Southern lights are an impressive sight at the Poles. They are caused by the collision of solar winds with the earth's magnetic field.

SEEKING NORTH!

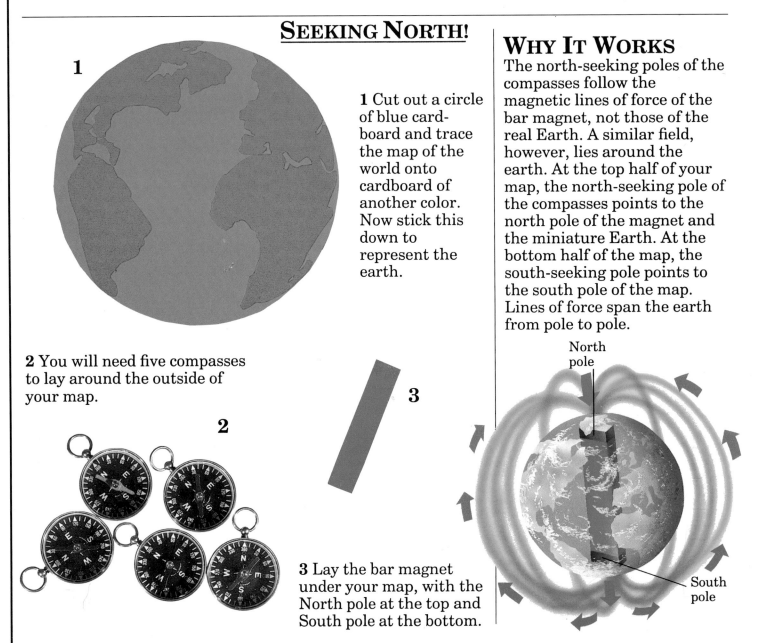

1 Cut out a circle of blue cardboard and trace the map of the world onto cardboard of another color. Now stick this down to represent the earth.

2 You will need five compasses to lay around the outside of your map.

3 Lay the bar magnet under your map, with the North pole at the top and South pole at the bottom.

WHY IT WORKS

The north-seeking poles of the compasses follow the magnetic lines of force of the bar magnet, not those of the real Earth. A similar field, however, lies around the earth. At the top half of your map, the north-seeking pole of the compasses points to the north pole of the magnet and the miniature Earth. At the bottom half of the map, the south-seeking pole points to the south pole of the map. Lines of force span the earth from pole to pole.

North pole

South pole

BRIGHT IDEAS

Place a compass on top of a map of your locality. Establish where magnetic north is, then rotate the map until north on the map is lined up with the north-seeking point of the compass needle. This is called orienting a map. In which direction are east, south, and west in relation to north?

North-seeking point

Compass

North

South

Magnet

South-seeking point

4 Position each compass as shown here, with north on the compass pointing north. The compass needle will move to follow the lines of force of the magnetic field of the bar magnet. Like the earth, these are said to travel from the North Pole to the South Pole.

4

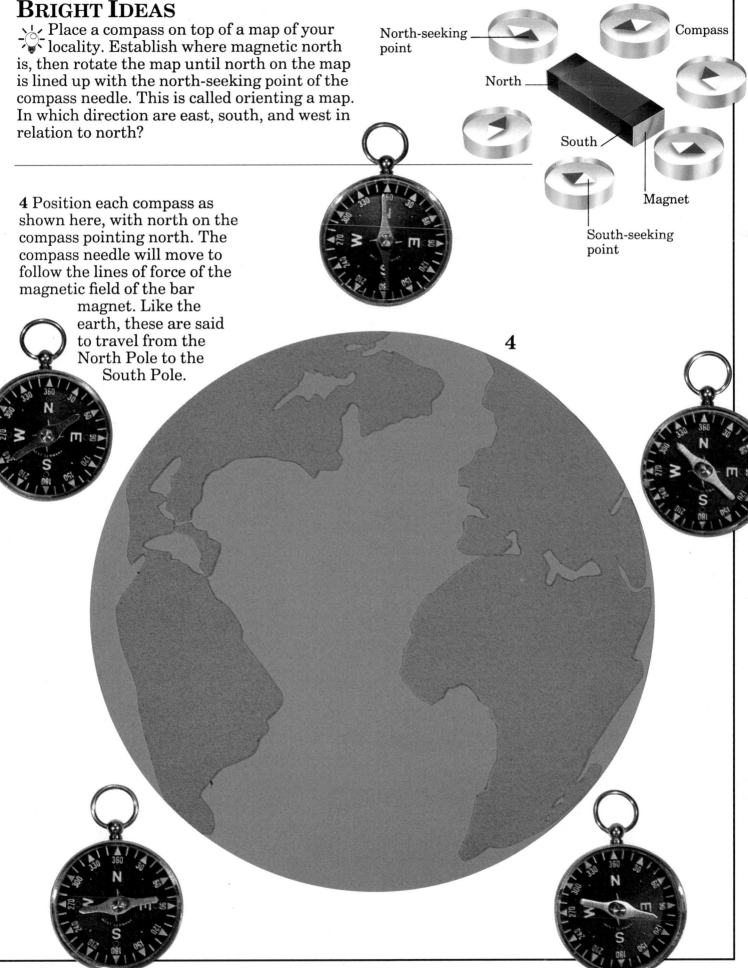

FOLLOWING MAGNETS

Almost 2,000 years ago, the Chinese knew how to make a simple compass by suspending a long, thin piece of magnetite or lodestone. Later, sailors used a lodestone to magnetize the needle for a ship's compass. Compasses were being used in China in the eleventh century. The Italian explorer, Amerigo Vespucci, whose name was mistakenly given to America, understood the concept of a magnetic North Pole. It was not until the sixteenth century, however, that it was fully accepted. Christopher Columbus was unable to navigate with total accuracy, because his compass readings were inaccurate – probably due to magnetic interference. Today, many large ships have a gyrocompass. This gives a bearing (compass direction) in relation to true north. Make your own simple compass by magnetizing a needle.

CRAFT A COMPASS

1 You will need a waterproof plate, a cork, a magnet, and a steel needle. Half fill the plate with clean water. Holding the magnet the same way all the time, stroke the needle with it at least 50 times. Always stroke in the same direction and lift the magnet off the needle each time you want to begin another stroke.

2 The needle has now been magnetized permanently, because it is steel. Push it through the cork so that the cork balances on the water evenly. Allow the water to become absolutely still. The needle will seek out the earth's magnetic North Pole to point north. Make sure there are no magnetic materials nearby.

2

1

WHY IT WORKS

By stroking a permanent magnet along the needle, the domains inside become aligned. This turns the needle into a magnet, too. Any magnet free to turn horizontally will settle pointing north/south, as the north-seeking pole is attracted to the earth's magnetic North Pole.

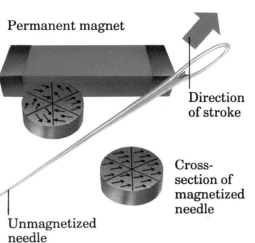

Permanent magnet

Direction of stroke

Unmagnetized needle

Cross-section of magnetized needle

BRIGHT IDEAS

Find a way to mark your compass clearly with the four compass directions. You could even design a compass rose.

Make a different kind of compass by pivoting a magnetized needle on folded cardboard on top of a stick. The stick is kept upright inside a container using modeling clay.

Place a paper clip underneath a metal lid made from a magnetic metal. Try to move the paper clip from beneath the lid with a magnet. You will find it difficult. Why is this?

Using a bar magnet you can show how a compass needle seeks out north. Suspend the magnet freely - make sure there are no magnets nearby - the magnet will rotate until it points north-south. The north-seeking pole (which is the south pole of the magnet) will face north.

Try floating a bar magnet on wood or cork in a bowl of water. What do you expect to happen?

Draw an eight-point compass. What is the size of the angle between each compass point?

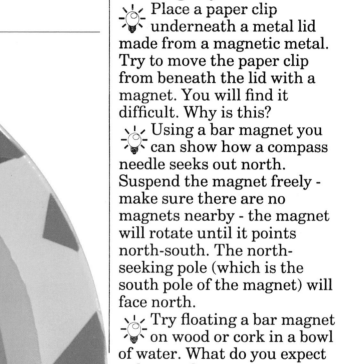

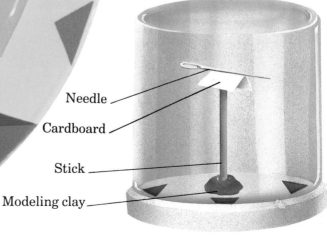

Plastic container

Needle

Cardboard

Stick

Modeling clay

ELECTROMAGNETS

The discovery of electromagnets in the 1800s was the first step in investigating the relationship between electricity and magnetism. In 1820, a Danish physicist, Hans Christian Oersted, discovered that a wire conducting an electric current produces a surrounding magnetic field. We now know that when electricity flows through a coil of wire wrapped around a soft iron core it creates a strong magnet, called an electromagnet. Electromagnets are used in many appliances and machines. Doorbells, telephones, and burglar alarms are only a few. The most powerful electromagnets are those used in scrapyards to lift heavy pieces of metal. You can build your own pickup using an electromagnet.

A MAGNETIC PICKUP

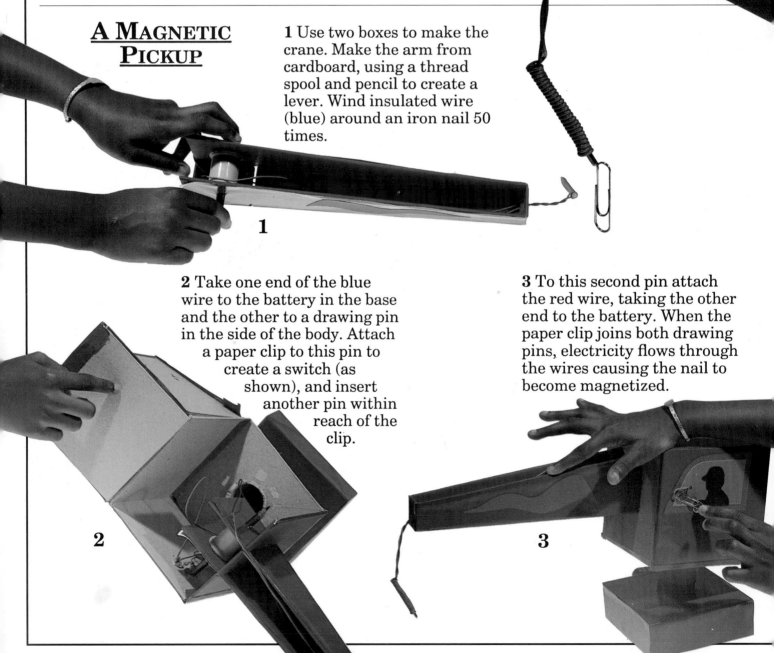

1 Use two boxes to make the crane. Make the arm from cardboard, using a thread spool and pencil to create a lever. Wind insulated wire (blue) around an iron nail 50 times.

2 Take one end of the blue wire to the battery in the base and the other to a drawing pin in the side of the body. Attach a paper clip to this pin to create a switch (as shown), and insert another pin within reach of the clip.

3 To this second pin attach the red wire, taking the other end to the battery. When the paper clip joins both drawing pins, electricity flows through the wires causing the nail to become magnetized.

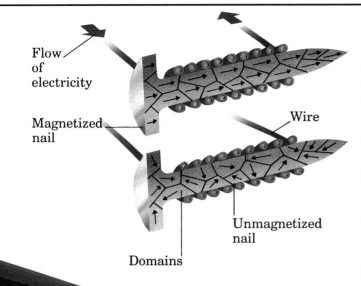

Flow
of
electricity

Magnetized
nail

Wire

Unmagnetized
nail

Domains

WHY IT WORKS

An electromagnet is a coil of wire around an iron core. When an electric current flows through the coil a strong magnetic field is created. The strength of the field depends upon the "push" of the current – the voltage. The strength of an electromagnet can be increased by the addition of extra turns of wire to the coil, by increasing the voltage in the circuit and by bringing the poles of the magnet closer together. If steel and not iron is used the metal will stay permanently magnetized. Iron becomes a temporary magnet. This means that when the current is switched off, the magnetic field disappears.

BRIGHT IDEAS

Wind about 60 turns of insulated wire around a steel nail. Connect the end to the battery and turn on the power. You have made a magnet. Make extra turns in the wire around the nail. Add another battery to the circuit. Observe any changes.

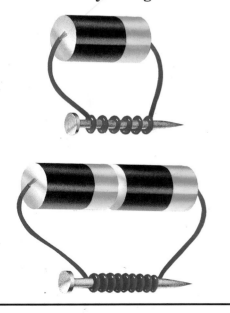

ELECTRICITY & MAGNETISM

During the 1800s, many people believed that magnetism could cure the sick. Franz Mesmer, a doctor, practiced conveying "animal magnetism" to his patients by gazing into their faces. The American scientist, Joseph Henry, discovered a more practical use for magnetism when he developed an even more powerful electromagnet. It was also discovered that electrical energy could be converted to mechanical energy by using a cylindrical coil of wire called a solenoid. This principle was later employed by Michael Faraday (pictured right) when he built his simple electric motor (see page 24). Make your own solenoid and watch the mouse hide in the cheese.

HIDE AND PEEP

1

1 Make a "wedge of cheese" with three square pieces of cardboard and two triangular sides. Color it yellow and hinge the sides to give access to the inside.

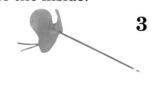

3

2 Through the triangular door insert wires connected to a battery. Coil the wire around a straw at least twenty times. Secure the straw on modeling clay inside the trap, making a hole in the side opposite.

2

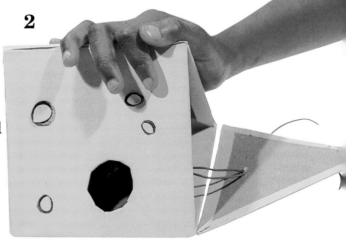

3 Attach a cardboard mouse's head to a needle. Make sure the head of the mouse will fit through the hole next to the straw.

WHY IT WORKS

An electric current is made up of tiny invisible particles, called electrons. When an electric current is passed through a wire it creates a magnetic field. This magnetic field becomes very strong when the wire is coiled many times around the straw. This solenoid acts as an electromagnet, pulling the needle inside the straw when the electric current is switched on.

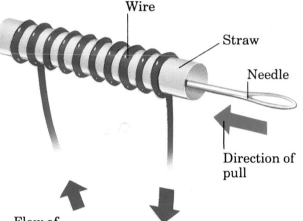

Wire

Straw

Needle

Direction of pull

Flow of electricity

BRIGHT IDEAS

Make the solenoid even stronger by winding more turns of wire on to the coil. See what happens when the current is turned off. Can your mouse peep out of the cheese again?

Remove the needle from the solenoid and test it for magnetization. See if it can pick up paper clips. Is it a temporary or permanent magnet?

Reconstruct Oersted's first experiment to show how a compass needle is deflected by the magnetic field produced by an electric current. Magnetize a needle and rest it on top of a piece of paper balanced on a stick (see page 19). Pass a wire carrying an electric current over the "compass," making sure there are no magnets nearby. Now repeat the experiment, winding coils of wire around a real compass.

4

4 Place the end of the needle into the straw leaving the mouse to peep outside. Connect the electric circuit. The mouse will duck back into the cheese.

MAGNETS & MOVEMENT

Electric motors use magnets to turn electricity into movement. In 1821 Michael Faraday developed the electric motor. He discovered that continuous motion could be produced by passing an electric current through a conductor in a strong magnetic field. Electrical appliances like washing machines and vacuum cleaners have electric motors. The TGV, one of France's most powerful trains, is powered by electric motors. An electric motor is a coil turning between the two poles of a permanent magnet. When current flows through the coil, a magnetic field is produced that turns the rotor. This movement is converted into electricity. A generator that powers bicycle lights (right) works on this principle.

SPIN THE COMPASS

1 Position two batteries with opposite terminals touching and hold them in place with paper and tape.

2 Wind a long length of insulated wire around a cardboard core at least 50 times – this could be a slice of cardboard tube. Leave two ends free to connect to the battery.

3 Attach the coil of wire to the base with tape. You have made a solenoid. Also attach the batteries.

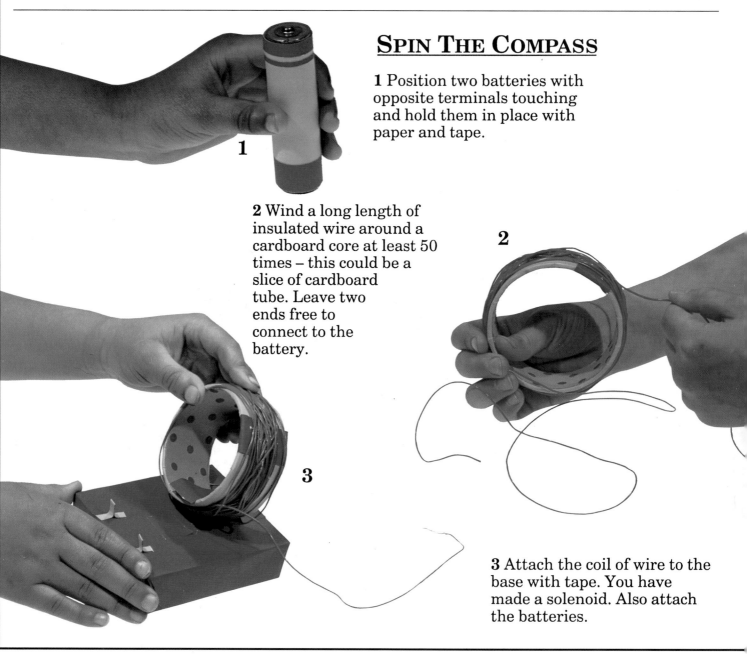

WHY IT WORKS

The magnetic field created by the electric current through the coil is strong enough to move the compass needle. When the current is turned on and off rapidly, the compass needle spins around continuously. The wire is copper. It is not magnetic and it does not affect the compass. When the electricity is turned on, each turn of wire has its own magnetic field. It is called a solenoid. A simple electric motor is a coil of wire mounted on a rod, so that it can rotate in a magnetic field. A current is passed into and out of the coil. An electric motor is clean and quiet.

BRIGHT IDEAS

☀ A simple electric motor like the one pictured here can be found in toy cars, hair dryers, and power drills. Maybe you could open up a broken toy and have a look?

☀ Recreate Faraday's experiment to illustrate the reverse principle - how a magnet can induce an electric current. You will need a small compass, placed inside a box. Wind at least 20 turns of wire around the box; at the other end of the wire you need a coil of at least 50 turns. Slowly pass a bar magnet through the coil and observe the compass.

Electric motor

North pole

Direction of rotation

Rotor

South pole

Electric current

4

4 Place a compass inside the coil. Connect the wires to the battery and observe the effect on the compass needle. Now connect and disconnect the wires repeatedly. Notice what happens to the compass needle.

USING MAGNETISM

The magnets used by scientists vary in size, shape, and strength. With the development of electricity, the electromagnet is now part of much modern equipment, both scientific and domestic. Numerous gadgets and machines work for us because of magnetism. They range from a lid-holding can opener to an atom-smashing machine, called a particle accelerator. In our homes, weak magnets help to hold refrigerator doors firmly shut. In factories, magnetic conveyor belts transport iron and steel cans. Precision instruments may have lightweight moving parts suspended inside them with a magnet. We all make use of machines like the ticket machines pictured here. They can sort coins into their different values. You can also sort coins using your own magnetic slot machine.

A MAGNETIC SLOT MACHINE

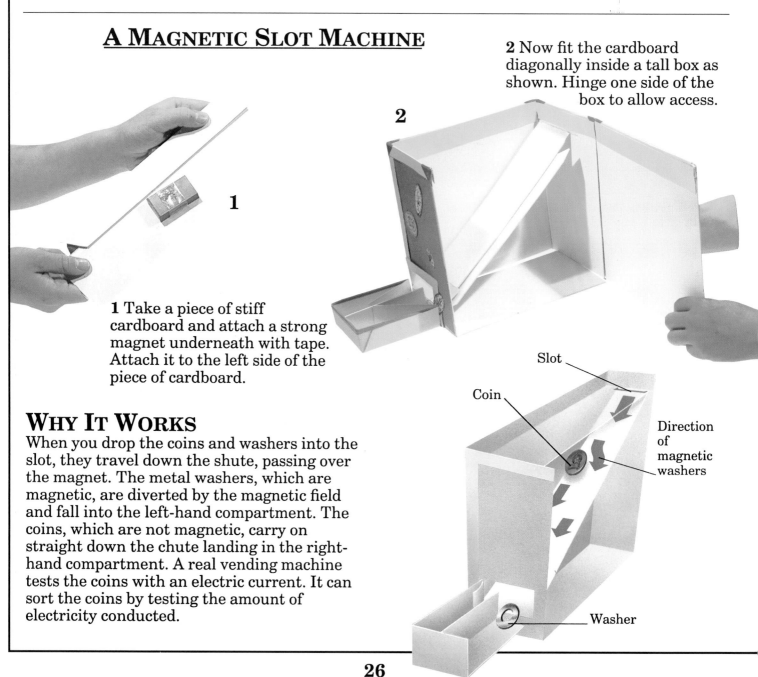

1 Take a piece of stiff cardboard and attach a strong magnet underneath with tape. Attach it to the left side of the piece of cardboard.

2 Now fit the cardboard diagonally inside a tall box as shown. Hinge one side of the box to allow access.

Slot

Coin

Direction of magnetic washers

Washer

WHY IT WORKS
When you drop the coins and washers into the slot, they travel down the shute, passing over the magnet. The metal washers, which are magnetic, are diverted by the magnetic field and fall into the left-hand compartment. The coins, which are not magnetic, carry on straight down the chute landing in the right-hand compartment. A real vending machine tests the coins with an electric current. It can sort the coins by testing the amount of electricity conducted.

BRIGHT IDEAS

☀ If you push the "coins" through the slot with greater force does it make any difference? Examine your results and draw conclusions from them.

☀ With small button magnets you can make some magnetic stickers. Cut out letters or shapes and color them in. Use them to make a board game.

☀ Draw your own weather map on magnetic material and design some weather symbols that can be mounted on small magnets.

3 Cut an opening at the bottom of the box, the same width as the stiff cardboard. Attach a cardboard tray divided into sections, as shown. Enclose the top of the box, cutting a slit adjacent to the top of the stiff, sloping cardboard. Make the slit long enough to allow coins to be pushed through.

3

4 Finish off your machine by decorating the outside. Collect as many different coins and metal washers as you can and roll each through the machine.

FLOATING MAGNETS

You have already learned that like poles repel and unlike poles attract. This principle has been adapted and used in industry and the world of transportation. In factories and other places where steel sheets need to be lifted, magnetic floaters, which are large permanent magnets, are placed on either side of steel sheets. They magnetize the steel and cause poles to form in adjacent parts of the sheets. As the like poles repel one another they cause the top sheet to lift off the pile. Electromagnets can create a moving magnetic field. The Maglev train (pictured above) works on this principle. The Maglev has no wheels – it is levitated along the track as two magnetic fields repel each other.

LEVITATION

1

3

2 The cutout magician is secured to a cardboard window that is the same size as the back of the box. Slide the magician inside the box so that he stands behind the magnet, touching it.

1 You will need a cardboard box wide enough to hold a bar magnet, two strong bar magnets, cardboard, and tape. Cut away one side of the box and fold back a second side to give access to the "stage." Attach two strips of cardboard to the floor wide enough to hold one of the bar magnets in place. Position the North pole of the magnet to the left side of the stage when you are facing it.

2

3 Cover the sides with fabric to look like curtains. To the second magnet attach a cardboard cutout "assistant," as shown. Ensure that the head of the figure is positioned at the North pole of the magnet.

WHY IT WORKS

Magnets can push as well as pull. The strongest part of a magnetic field is at the poles and like poles repel. As both ends of the magnets repel each other, the top magnet is able to float above the other. It is important to support the top magnet at the sides so it cannot be pushed off in one direction.

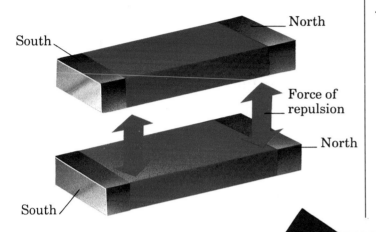

South — North

Force of repulsion

North

South

BRIGHT IDEAS

Place some balsa wood between two magnets with opposite poles facing each other. Tape them together at each end and remove the wood. Press down on the top magnet. You will feel the "spring" of repulsion. This is how the Maglev train works.

Get some small ring magnets and arrange them along a pencil. Place them so that they repel each other and see them float.

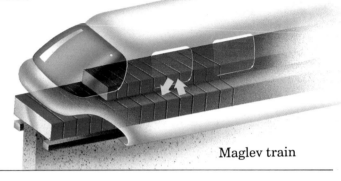

Maglev train

4

4 Place a small pencil or a piece of wood across the magnet on the floor of the stage. Gently position the "assistant" on top of it, parallel with the first magnet. Her head should be on the left. You may need to tape the ends of the two magnets together. Carefully remove the pencil and watch the lady levitate.

FUN WITH MAGNETS

Now that you know more about magnets, how many do you think you could find around your home and school? Maybe you have refrigerator magnets or a magnetic notice board. Somebody you know may have a magnetic catch on their bag or maybe you own a magnetic travel game like chess or checkers. If you want them to be, magnets can be lots of fun. But you must take care of them! All magnets become weaker over time and should be stored carefully, in pairs, with unlike poles together. Every magnet should have a piece of soft iron, called a keeper, across each end. Be careful not to drop your magnets, as this can result in their losing their magnetic powers. Magnetic sculptures can be bought in stores, but you can make your own with paper clips. Gather together your magnets and have some fun!

MAGNETIC SCULPTURE

Place a bar magnet beneath an upturned paper plate. Gather together some paper clips and scatter them on top of the plate. The magnetic field of the magnet travels through the plate, magnetizing the paper clips. Now you can build up a sculpture, making all kinds of different shapes. How high can you build? See what happens when you take the magnet away.

BEARDED FACE

Draw and color in a man's face on a paper plate. Leave out his hair, eyebrows, and moustache. Now place some iron filings on the plate. Keeping the plate level, lift it in one hand and hold a magnet underneath with the other. By moving the magnet around under the plate, you can make hair grow. You could even create a hair-raising monster! To make another picture, just remove the magnet and shake.

BUZZING BEE

To suspend your buzzing bee, join two sticks together with tape, as shown. Make a hole in an upturned flowerpot and insert the longest stick.

Cut a Ping Pong ball in half and paint the bee's stripes. Add some wings, eyes, and antennae.

Now take a bar magnet and cover it in brown paper. Stand it upright in the center of your base, securing it with modeling clay. This will be your flower stem.

Suspend the bee from the pole with a piece of thread, and attach a button magnet inside the body with modeling clay.

Cut out some petals from colored paper and make a large flower, as shown.

Suspend your bee from the pole so that it hangs just above the flower. Watch the bee buzz around the flower. Once in motion, it will continue to fly as it is repeatedly attracted and repelled by the bar magnet in the stem. Notice if there is any pattern to the bee's buzzing. What if you turn the bar magnet the other way up? Does the pattern change?

SCIENTIFIC TERMS

ELECTRIC MOTOR A machine that uses a magnet to to turn electricity into movement.

ELECTROMAGNETISM The relationship between electricity and magnetism – one can be used to produce the other.

GYROCOMPASS A compass that points to true North because it does not use magnetism.

LODESTONE A piece of magnetite; a magnetic rock used as a compass by early explorers.

MAGNETIC FIELD The area surounding a magnet or an electric current that attracts or repels magnetic materials.

MAGNETIC INDUCTION Making a temporary magnet out of a magnetic material by placing it within the magnetic field of a permanent magnet.

MAGNETIC NORTH POLE The point on the earth's surface where magnetism is concentrated. The magnetic north pole is about 1,000 miles (1,600 km) from the geographic North Pole.

MAGNETIC SHIELD A magnetic material placed within a magnetic field to cancel out the effect of another magnet.

MAGNETISM An invisible force that attracts or repels magnetic materials.

MAGNETIZE Making a magnet by stroking or touching a magnetic material with a permanent magnet.

MAGNETOMETER An instrument for measuring the direction or intensity of a magnetic field.

NEUTRAL POINT The point where two opposing magnetic fields cancel each other out as a result of the repulsion of like poles.

SOLENOID A cylindrical coil of wire that acts as a magnet when an electric currrent is passed through it.

INDEX